CASTING
~the~
RUNES
ᛒᛏᛟ **CARD PACK** ᛉᛁᛘ

JON TREMAINE

UNLOCK THE ANCIENT CRAFT OF SELF-PREDICTION

STEWART
TABORI
& CHANG

A GODSFIELD PRESS PRODUCTION

Copyright © 1996 Godsfield Press

Text © 1996 Jon Tremaine

Illustration © 1996 Helen Holroyd

Written by Jon Tremaine

Published in 1996 and distributed in the U.S. by

Stewart, Tabori and Chang, a division of U.S. Media Holdings, Inc.

575 Broadway, New York, New York 10012.

Distributed in Canada by General Publishing Co. Ltd.

30 Lesmill Road, Don Mills, Ontario, Canada, M3B 2T6.

ISBN: 1-55670-503-4

First Edition

Printed and bound in China

10 9 8 7 6 5 4 3 2 1

DESIGNED AND PRODUCED BY

THE BRIDGEWATER BOOK COMPANY LTD

CONTENTS

THE ORIGIN AND MEANING OF RUNES

When people first began to communicate with each other in a written rather than an oral way, they did so using simple drawings that they scratched upon cave walls and trees. Their history and culture were recorded in this way.

The ancient Egyptians developed this form of communication into an art form, which can still be seen to this day on the walls of the pyramids.

Similarly, the Rune alphabet was developed by our Scandinavian/Germanic ancestors and can be traced back to the second century B.C. Runic symbols look very similar to ancient carvings from the Stone Age and may have evolved from these shapes.

According to Norse mythology, the god Odin, in an effort to learn the secrets of life and death, hung himself upside down from the world-ash tree (Yggdrasil), impaled by his own spear. During

An engraved Rune stone from the seventh century

this ordeal, tormented by pain, hunger, and thirst, he spied some Runes below him and seized them. Afterward he passed on the secrets of the Runes to mankind.

In ancient times, literacy was a rarity and was not taken for granted as it is today. Runemasters – those capable of carving and reading Runic inscriptions – became highly respected members of society and were looked upon with awe and reverence. Because the northern tribes were nomadic, the Runemasters transferred the symbols to small stones and wooden, bone, and clay slabs, to make them easier to carry.

Each Rune is a pictorial representation of a particular natural mood or condition. The name of each Rune has been chosen with care, because it has to begin with a particular sound. Notice how angular the Rune symbols are. This is probably due to the limitations placed on the carver by the tools available at the time: straight lines were easier to carve.

We can make some comparisons with the Roman alphabet that is used by most European countries, because the shapes are similar in some ways. Each Rune has a keyword, a meaning, a deity, a color, a tree, a herb, a polarity, and a specific Element attributed to it. Some Runes also have an associated bird or animal.

In the Old Norse language the word "Run" means "secret writing." In Gothic the word "Runa" means a "secret" or a "whisper." In Old English we find the word "Roun," and in German the word "Raunen." So all these languages agree that the Runes reveal "whispered secrets."

We can see, then, that the Runes should not be regarded simply as a fortune-telling instrument. They are

The goddess Freya is associated with several of the Runes

greater than that. The Runes are an oracle that is, in many ways, more subtle than the amazing Chinese oracle, the I Ching.

The Runes pinpoint your hidden fears and the unseen influences that affect your future. The interpretation of a Rune cast will in no way absolve you from the responsibility of choice. It will, however, point out the alternatives to a course of action. The Runes are, in every way, a constructive medium. They describe the positive forces that are working on your behalf – for your own good. Runes will point out bad influences too, but they will always suggest positive actions that will help reverse the adverse forces.

Let the strength of the Runes become *your* strength. Have complete faith in them. Your commitment will be rewarded.

HOW TO USE
THE RUNE PACK

he Rune Pack contains a book and a pack of 25 cards that are designed to be used together to enable you to pinpoint your hidden fears and desires and influence your own future.

This book uses the oldest Scandinavian/Germanic version of the Runic alphabet, known as Futhark, because it derives its name from the sound of the first six letters:
F (Fehu)   U (Uruz)   Th (Thurisaz)
A (Ansuz)   R (Raido)   K (Kaunaz)

The 24 main Runes are divided into three sets of eight (see page 64), each set being dedicated to a Norse god. Thus we have Freyr's Aett, Hagal's Aett and Tyr's Aett. Then there is the mysterious 25th Rune, known as Wyrd. It has no symbol – just a blank face – and some experts dismiss its inclusion, believing that the *true* Rune of Fate is Pertho.

Results will not come right away. You have to work at reading the Runes, and use your intuitive intelligence to interpret how one Rune relates to another. You may find it helpful to keep a Runic diary recording your progress and interpretations.

Your procedure before each reading should always be the same. Clear your mind of everything except the question or problem that concerns you. Try to formulate your question in a clear, succinct way. Shuffle the Rune cards thoroughly, then hold them cupped in your hands for a few quiet moments while your personal vibrations are absorbed by the cards – then proceed as directed by the Rune casting that you are following. Avoid the temptation to ask more than one question during the same session. If your interpretation of the Rune cast seems to contradict itself, it is a sign that the time is not right to consult the Runes and that the outcome is probably in the lap of the gods. Try again tomorrow.

The information on page 13 shows you how to make and cast on a Runic cloth or casting board, and how to reveal the elemental influence that refines each Rune.

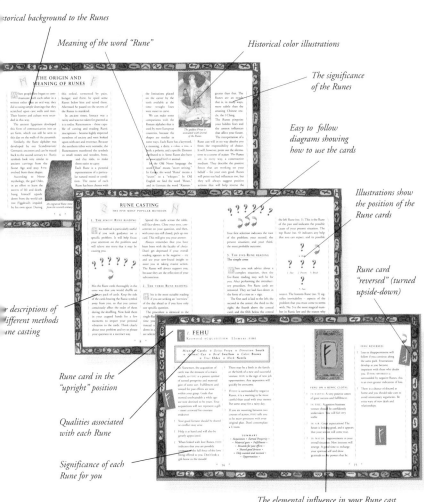

Historical background to the Runes

Meaning of the word "Rune"

Historical color illustrations

The significance of the Runes

Easy to follow diagrams showing how to use the cards

Illustrations show the position of the Rune cards

Rune card "reversed" (turned upside-down)

Fuller descriptions of the different methods of Rune casting

Rune card in the "upright" position

Qualities associated with each Rune

Significance of each Rune for you

The elemental influence in your Rune cast

RUNE CASTING

1. THE SINGLE-RUNE READING

his method is particularly useful if you seek guidance on a specific problem. It will help focus your attention on the problem and will relieve any stress that it may be causing you.

Mix the Rune cards thoroughly in the same way that you would shuffle an ordinary pack of cards. Keep the side of the cards bearing the Runic symbol away from you, so that you cannot consciously affect the order of them during the shuffling. Now hold them in your cupped hands for a few moments to impart your personal vibration to the cards. Think clearly about your problem and try to phrase your question in a succinct way.

Spread the cards across the table, still face-down. Close your eyes, concentrate on your question, and then, with your eyes still closed, pick up one card. This will give you your answer.

Always remember that you have been born with the faculty of *choice*. Don't get depressed if your overall reading appears to be negative – try and use your new-found insight to assist you in taking evasive action. The Runes will always support you, because they are the reflection of your subconscious.

2. THE THREE-RUNE READING

his is the most suitable reading if you are seeking an "overview" of the day ahead or if you have only one specific question.

The procedure is identical to the single-Rune reading except that this time you select three Rune cards instead of one. They are laid face-down in a row from *left to right* as they are selected. Then turn them over.

Your first selection indicates the root of the problem; your second, the present situation; and your third, the most probable outcome.

3. THE FIVE-RUNE READING
The simple cross

When you seek advice about a complex situation, then the five-Rune reading may well be for you. After performing the introductory procedure, five Rune cards are removed. They are laid face-down in the form of a cross or + sign.

The first card is laid to the left; the second in the center; the third to the right; the fourth above the central card; and the fifth below the central card. Read them in a 2 - 1 - 4 - 5 - 3 order. Turn over the center Rune first (no. 2). This depicts your present situation. It shows what the problem is and how you regard it. Then turn over

the left Rune (no. 1). This is the Rune of the past and indicates the possible cause of your present situation. The top Rune (no. 4) indicates any help that you can expect, and its possible

4. *Help*

1. *Past*   2. *Present*   3. *Result*

5. *Fate*

source. The bottom Rune (no. 5) signifies inevitability – aspects of the problem that you must come to terms with. No. 3 is the most magical number in Runic law and the reason why you leave the right-hand Rune until last. This is the "result" position. It reveals the most likely outcome of your Rune cast. Its revelations should hold good for up to eight weeks.

4. THE SIX-RUNE READING
The Runic cross

The layout is the same as for the five-Rune cross, but with an extra Rune card at the base of the cross and the last to be laid (sixth). This Rune represents fresh influences that could affect you. Follow the procedure for the five-Rune cross and read the "result" Rune (no. 3) last. So the order will be 2 - 1 - 4 - 5 - 6 - 3.

An ode to the King of the Goths inscribed on a ninth-century Rune stone

5. THE RUNIC WHEEL

After performing the introductory procedure, deal 12 Rune cards in a circle. Imagine a clock face – the first card goes at the nine o'clock position (we call this the First House), the second at the eight o'clock position (the Second House), and so on, anti-clockwise around the circle, until you have dealt the twelfth card at the ten o'clock position (the Twelfth House). Then deal a thirteenth Rune card into the center of the circle.

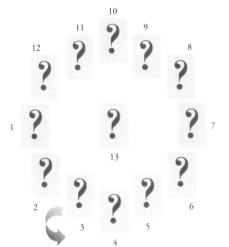

Turn all the cards face-up and commence your "reading" from the nine o'clock position, working in an anti-clockwise direction.

You may consider the Runic Wheel to represent either the next 12 days – the Runic symbols providing an overview of each particular day – or the next 12 months. Just decide which you want it to be *before* you commence the shuffling.

The center card represents the overall "feel" of the period in question and the person for whom the reading is intended. It should be considered last.

It may soften or harden the effects of any individual Rune card in the spread.

Each position is called a House and has its own specific meaning. Each Rune can also be considered in four separate ways depending on: 1) its own innate qualities; 2) how its meaning is qualified by the effect of its neighbors; 3) how it is affected by the influence of the center Rune; 4) how the particular House in which it resides affects the interpretation of the Rune.

A list of the 12 Houses and their meanings follows on page 12.

THE 12 HOUSES
AND THEIR MEANINGS

H O U S E 1 *(9 o'clock)* Self, the motivations of your actions, your general well-being and mental health

H O U S E 2 *(8 o'clock)* Material possessions, general finance, feelings toward partnerships of a business nature

H O U S E 3 *(7 o'clock)* Nonparental relatives, transportation, environmental affairs, education, and your ability to communicate

H O U S E 4 *(6 o'clock)* Your home, your nearest and dearest – especially your mother – domestic life in general

H O U S E 5 *(5 o'clock)* Creativity, pleasure, children, love affairs, risk-taking, paternal influences, and affairs

H O U S E 6 *(4 o'clock)* Health and how you treat your body, diet, exercise, hobbies, attitudes to routine work

H O U S E 7 *(3 o'clock)* Relationships of all kinds, your commitment to partnerships

H O U S E 8 *(2 o'clock)* Sex, inheritance, investments, possible deception, self-analysis

H O U S E 9 *(1 o'clock)* Ideals, dreams, long-distance travel, challenges, spiritual enlightenment

H O U S E 10 *(12 o'clock)* Ambitions and aspirations, authority and how you handle it, sense of duty, careers

H O U S E 11 *(11 o'clock)* Social life, social objectives, social conscience, friendships, and charitable works

H O U S E 12 *(10 o'clock)* Seclusion, escapism and inner contemplation, faith, personal sacrifices

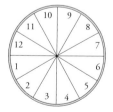

CASTING ON A
RUNIC CLOTH OR BOARD

When you have gained a little experience at interpreting the Runes, you may like to add a further dimension by making a Runic cloth. Alternatively, you can make a casting board, which will serve you just as well and also act as a template, if you decide to make a Runic cloth.

Buy a large white sheet of card-board from an artist's supply store and cut it into a square approximately 2 feet by 2 feet. Draw in the diagonals and, from this intersection, draw a circle 18 inches in diameter. Print the Elements Fire, Water, Air, and Earth as shown on the diagram and color the four segments in the "elemental colors"; red for Fire, black for Earth, yellow for Air and blue for Water.

If you do decide to make a Runic cloth, start with a square yard of white jersey silk material, which is very crease-resistant. White is recommended because it contrasts nicely with the four segments of the circle when embroidered with the elemental colors.

Place your Runic cloth or casting board on the table. Perform your Runic card preparation in the usual way. Then spread the cards at random all over the surface of the cloth or board. Pick up any 16 cards and put them to one side. Then, starting at the nine o'clock position and counting anticlockwise, discard every third Rune card until there are only three left on the cloth or board.

Turn the three remaining cards face-up and note in which of the four segments they lie. The basic meaning of each Rune is now further refined by the elemental influence that you have just revealed.

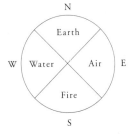

1. FEHU

Keyword: ACQUISITION Element: FIRE

> *Meaning:* **Cattle** ✳ *Deity:* **Freya** ✳ *Direction:* **South**
> ✳ *Animal:* **Cat** ✳ *Bird:* **Swallow** ✳ *Color:* **Brown**
> ✳ *Tree:* **Elder** ✳ *Herb:* **Nettle**

To Norsemen, the acquisition of cattle was the measure of a man's wealth, so FEHU is a potent symbol of earned prosperity and material gain of some sort. Fulfillment and reward for past efforts are now within your grasp. Goals that seemed unobtainable a while ago are now destined to be yours. Your acquisitions will not represent a gift – more a reward for constant endeavor.

Your good fortune should be shared or conflict may arise.

Help is at hand and will also be greatly appreciated.

When linked with love Runes, FEHU indicates that you are possibly unaware of the full force of the love being offered to you. Don't look a gift horse in the mouth!

There may be a birth in the family or the birth of a new and successful venture. FEHU is the sign of new job opportunities. Any opposition will quickly be overcome.

If FEHU is surrounded by negative Runes, it is a warning to be more careful than usual with your money. Put some away for a rainy day.

If you are wavering between two courses of action, FEHU tells you to be more persistent with your original plan. Don't contemplate a U-turn.

SUMMARY
* Acquisition * Earned Prosperity *
* Material gain * Fulfillment *
* Rewards for past efforts *
* Shared good fortune *
* Help wanted and received *
* Opportunities *

FEHU ON A RUNIC CLOTH:

ᚠ IN EARTH: A very positive omen of great success and fulfillment.

ᚠ IN FIRE: A positive business venture should be confidently undertaken. You will feel very stable.

ᚠ IN AIR: Great expectations! The future is looking good, and it appears that your wishes will come true.

ᚠ IN WATER: Improvements in your overall situation. New interests will emerge. A good time to recharge your spiritual self and show gratitude to the powers that be.

FEHU REVERSED:

ᚠ Loss or disappointment will follow if you continue along the same path. Frustrations develop as you become impatient with those who doubt you. If FEHU REVERSED is surrounded by negative Runes, this is an even greater indication of loss.

ᚠ There is a chance of discord at home and you should take care to avoid unnecessary arguments. Be extra wary of new deals and relationships.

2. URUZ

Keyword: POWER   Element: EARTH

Meaning: **Wild oxen** ✳ *Deity:* **Thor**
✳ *Direction:* **North** ✳ *Animal:* **Aurochs**
✳ *Color:* **Green** ✳ *Tree:* **Birch** ✳ *Herb:* **Moss**

◠ URUZ was the name given to the gigantic wild ox, later called the aurochs, which is now extinct. It was untameable, possessed great speed, courage, and strength.

◠ URUZ is, therefore, a symbol of strength, virility, vitality, good health, strong resistance, and quick recovery from illness.

◠ Strong emotions show and your enthusiasm is infectious! Utilize this quality by capitalizing on the willing support of your friends and associates.

◠ URUZ is also the sign of a strong will and sudden but favorable changes of a personal nature. Don't let your natural pride prevent you from taking advantage of genuine opportunities.

◠ Slow improvement in business matters is indicated, with a strong hint of promotion. You will probably find this a very emotional period in your life.

◠ URUZ often symbolizes our need to sort out the "cupboards of our life" – to do a bit of pruning – to make room for new ideas and adventures. The surrounding Runes in your cast will pinpoint the direction.

◠ If URUZ appears with positive Runes, it is an indication of success against all the odds!

SUMMARY
✳ *Strength* ✳ *Good health* ✳
✳ *Strong emotions* ✳ *Enthusiasm* ✳
✳ *Improvements* ✳ *Promotion* ✳
✳ *New ideas* ✳

URUZ ON A RUNIC CLOTH:

ᚾ IN EARTH: A time for extreme caution. You must look before you leap. Contain any unfounded or unreasonable enthusiasm.

ᚾ IN FIRE: A time to obey your intuition and forge bravely ahead. He who hesitates is lost.

ᚾ IN AIR: A very fortunate time for you. You will find many opportunities to advance your plans.

ᚾ IN WATER: An unexpected visitor, or perhaps a contact from afar, possibly from overseas.

URUZ REVERSED:

ᚸ You must be aware of the destructive forces around you that could cause you to fail.

ᚸ Be sparing with your trust at this time.

ᚸ You could benefit by strengthening your willpower because you appear to be too easily led.

ᚸ You seem listless at the moment and need to take more care of your health. URUZ REVERSED is often a warning of a potential minor illness. Avoid it by taking evasive action.

3. THURISAZ

Keyword: CHALLENGE   Element: FIRE

Meaning: **Giant** ✳ *Deity:* **Thor**
✳ *Direction:* **Southwest** ✳ *Animal:* **Snake**
✳ *Color:* **White** ✳ *Tree:* **Blackthorn** ✳ *Herb:* **Leek**

▷ The experts disagree about the exact meaning of THURISAZ – giant, troll, ice demon, or thorn? Take your pick!

▷ All recognize, however, that THURISAZ is a Rune of protection. I have found that it warns against headstrong action. It can also be the sign of unexpected good luck from an unlikely source! A case of "It's not what you know but who you know!"

▷ This indicates a time when you should definitely look before you leap. It is not a time for gambling on anything, but a definite sign that you should sit on the fence and not get involved.

▷ People may consider that you are being too self-opinionated, so pay more attention to the opinions of others. There is more than one way to skin a cat – yours might just be the wrong way at the moment.

▷ THURISAZ is a sign that very strong negative influences are working against you. They are being projected by people who are stronger than you, in every sense of the word. Don't oppose them, just step to one side, and their momentum will cause them to self-destruct. This is not the right time for you to pick a fight!

▷ THURISAZ is also symbolic of change. Any change that is offered to you, either on a business or

---

SUMMARY
* Protection * Good luck * Look before you leap * Difficult challenges * Negative influences *
* Changes afoot *

---

personal level, should be looked upon with suspicion and considered very carefully before being adopted or rejected.

THURISAZ ON A RUNIC CLOTH:

- IN EARTH: Avoid confrontation. Negotiate your way out of problems. Think before you act.

- IN FIRE: Think twice about every decision before you commit yourself. Watch out for those who may try to exploit the situation.

- IN AIR: Be patient. Don't take any unnecessary risks.

- IN WATER: Extreme caution is called for in every aspect of your life. New ventures and acquaintances should be looked upon with suspicion.

THURISAZ REVERSED:

- The above negative findings are slightly watered down when THURISAZ is in a reversed aspect.

I say "slightly" because it is still a somewhat negative symbol. It illustrates a strong temptation to avoid the warning signs and lunge ahead into an enterprise or relationship without giving it sufficient thought.

- Caution is called for, because THURISAZ REVERSED is not a particularly lucky indicator.

- Be careful to avoid self-deception. Be brutally honest with yourself, even at the risk of losing face.

4. ANSUZ

Keyword: KNOWLEDGE   Element: AIR

Meaning: **God** ✳ *Deity:* **Odin** ✳ *Direction:* **East**
✳ *Animal:* **Wolf** ✳ *Bird:* **Raven** ✳ *Color:* **Purple**
✳ *Tree:* **Ash** ✳ *Herb:* **Amanita muscaria**

ᚠ ANSUZ is a symbol of learning, communication, and creativity.

ᚠ You are under the protection of a Higher Force, and any advice that you receive, especially from an older person, should be acted upon, because the advice is freely given without thought of reward.

ᚠ This could be a time to pursue intellectual pursuits – possibly a course of further education – or even a completely new interest.

ᚠ This is a wonderful period in your life because you are protected by the ANSUZ influence. You could call this "divine protection." The sun certainly seems to be shining on you at the moment, and everything that you turn your hand to seems to work out to your advantage. This is because the advice that you have been given (and should act upon) is based on personal experience.

ᚠ A spiritual awareness is indicated, which brings blessings and renewed faith.

SUMMARY
∗ *Knowledge* ∗ *Communication* ∗
∗ *Creativity* ∗ *Intellectual pursuits* ∗
∗ *New interests* ∗
∗ *Divine protection* ∗
∗ *Spiritual awareness* ∗

ANSUZ ON A RUNIC CLOTH:

IN EARTH: Plan ahead now. Make provisions for your future. Reassess your responsibilities and honor them.

IN FIRE: A time to cooperate and seek the advice of others who are older and wiser than you. Heed any advice that they give you.

IN AIR: A surprise meeting could turn out to be very fortunate for you.

IN WATER: Your motives could be misunderstood – so seek help from those who know your intentions and have your well-being at heart.

ANSUZ REVERSED:

All the interpretations of ANSUZ are negated when the sign is reversed. This is not necessarily an intimation that you are approaching a bad period. It merely means that you must be ever-watchful for the lies, trickery, and general deceit that may come your way from an older person.

Get a second or even a third opinion if the outcome of your problem is of great importance to you. Most of your problems at this time are due to misunderstanding and lack of communication.

Disruptive influences could also be attempting to interfere with your plans.

5. **RAIDO**

Keyword: TRAVEL   Element: AIR

> *Meaning:* **Wagon** ✳ *Deity:* **Tyr**
> ✳ *Direction:* **East** ✳ *Animal:* **Goat** ✳ *Color:* **Black**
> ✳ *Tree:* **Oak** ✳ *Herb:* **Mugwort**

ᚱ The original meaning of RAIDO was "wagon" or "chariot." Consequently this Rune deals with travel, in both a physical and a spiritual way.

ᚱ The journey will be for pleasure and could be accompanied by agreeable companions. It will be a safe, painless excursion!

ᚱ RAIDO signifies a good period for discussions and negotiations. Ask for that raise, sell the house, buy those new clothes! If your question is concerned with acquisitions of either a physical or spiritual nature, RAIDO advice is positive.

ᚱ It also signifies a reunion. This could mean renewed friendship or renewed faith.

ᚱ A message of a surprising, pleasant nature could be forthcoming.

ᚱ You are warned to curb any excesses in your life and to think a little less of your material wealth and more of your spiritual wealth.

ᚱ If you cannot decide between two courses of action, look at the surrounding Runes. If they are negative, you should beware of the advice of others.

ᚱ Any legal matters should be approached in a positive manner because the signs are good for a favorable outcome.

> **SUMMARY**
> * Travel * Agreeable companions *
> * Discussions * Negotiations *
> * Reunions * Messages *
> * Curb any excesses *
> * Favorable legal activity *

RAIDO ON A RUNIC CLOTH:

ᚱ IN EARTH: Not a time to take chances. Progress will be slow but sure. Welcome surprises are possible.

ᚱ IN FIRE: Take care in your decision-making. Take advice from those near and dear to you. Caution is called for.

ᚱ IN AIR: Don't take things so seriously. Lighten up and retain a sense of humor.

ᚱ IN WATER: Discretion is called for. This is a time to keep a secret and to avoid gossip. Play your cards close to your chest!

RAIDO REVERSED:

ᚱ Pay particular attention to personal relationships. Your loved ones may be feeling a little unwanted and you should reassure them that you love them, too.

ᚱ Strive to keep your sense of humor because you could be sorely tried. You will not find it easy to keep the peace.

ᚱ Your travel plans show signs of disruption and they may well have to be redrawn. Try to take a philosophical approach to these frustrations.

6. KENAZ

Keyword: ENLIGHTENMENT   Element: FIRE

Meaning: **Torch** ✳ *Deity:* **Frey** ✳ *Direction:* **South**
✳ *Bird:* **Night owl** ✳ *Color:* **Yellow**
✳ *Tree:* **Pine** ✳ *Herb:* **Cowslip**

‹ This is the sign of the controlled, friendly, and warm fire of the flaming torch.

‹ KENAZ is therefore is an indication of strength and boundless energy. Your mental and physical powers will be at their most telling, enabling you to achieve great things that were previously beyond your grasp.

‹ Health will no longer be a problem and, if you have recently suffered an illness, the time is right for you to make a rapid and complete recovery. This could just as easily refer to a "sick" project, which can now be brought to a successful conclusion.

‹ KENAZ means that this is a time for positive action to counteract the nagging aggravations that have been concerning you. Any opposition to your wishes will be quickly and painlessly swept away.

‹ Prepare to accept new ideas. This is a most creative time for you, as you see the end of a "dull" period. An exciting future lies ahead.

‹ KENAZ often signifies birth. Once again, this may be physical or mental. Sexual energy and the regeneration of ideas can be tempered and molded by the flaming torch of this Rune.

S U M M A R Y
* *Strength* * *Energy* * *Great achievements* * *Recuperation* *
* *Positive action* * *New concepts* *
* *Exciting outlook* * *Regeneration* *

KENAZ ON A RUNIC CLOTH:

‹ IN EARTH: General improvement in your happiness. Your mind and body will benefit from renewed health and strength.

‹ IN FIRE: The future is looking extremely promising. Make sure that you recognize your opportunities when they present themselves.

‹ IN AIR: Assistance is on the way that could result in a surprising material gain. Don't look a gift horse in the mouth!

‹ IN WATER: A very advantageous period for you, which you should not be ashamed of exploiting!

KENAZ REVERSED:

› You must face up to the changes that may be happening in your life and fight for the things that you hold dear.

› This is a time for realism and critical self-examination.

› You could miss out on a golden opportunity by your complacency.

› Do not be hasty in your decision-making, because this could involve you in wasted time and energy.

7. GEBO

Keyword: PARTNERSHIP   Element: AIR

Meaning: **A gift** ✳ *Deity:* **Odin**
✳ *Direction:* **East** ✳ *Animal:* **Oxen** ✳ *Color:* **Red**
✳ *Tree:* **Elm** ✳ *Herb:* **Pansy**

X This is one of the most positive of all the Runes. It is too positive to have a reversed aspect!

X The meaning of GEBO is "a gift," and it bestows good fortune on you in every way. If it appears in the "result" position in your Rune cast, then success and happiness are assured.

X GEBO is a sign of partnership – especially in the "sharing" interpretation of the word. It could signify an extremely favorable marriage, either of a romantic or business nature. Certainly an important development is imminent in this direction.

X GEBO suggests that you should open your purse-strings or wallet and give generously to those less fortunate than yourself. Open your heart to the plight of others and assist them with your contribution to their future well-being.

X People around you may not live by the same rules as you. They may not share your values. GEBO warns you to be tolerant and to appreciate the free will of others. Do your best to accommodate the time-consuming requests that may be showered upon you.

X You could receive recognition and rewards for your past endeavors. A lucky sign – a lucky time!

SUMMARY
* *Good fortune* * *Success* *
* *Happiness* * *Partnership* *
* *Sharing* * *Favorable emotional period* * *Recognition* *
* *Tolerance called for* *

GEBO ON A RUNIC CLOTH:

X **IN EARTH:** A time to increase your efforts and forge ahead, in the knowledge that you are proceeding along the right path and that success is assured.

X **IN FIRE:** Your romantic wishes will be fulfilled and your desires will be satisfied. You are surrounded by love.

X **IN AIR:** Seek out that almost forgotten friend. Renew old contacts. Avoid being alone at this time. You *have* friends – share yourself with them now!

X **IN WATER:** You need a helping hand. Your friends are anxious and willing to guide and enlighten you. Accept their generous gift.

X **GEBO** has no reversed aspect.

8. WUNJO

Keyword: BLISS   Element: EARTH

Meaning: **Joy or perfection** ＊ *Deity:* **Odin**
＊ *Direction:* **North** ＊ *Color:* **Blue**
＊ *Tree:* **Ash** ＊ *Herb:* **Flax**

WUNJO is very good news in many ways! In business matters and personal relationships this Rune signifies contentment and ultimate achievement. It is extremely positive. Aims that have long eluded you are finally and triumphantly realized. For those considered to be artistically gifted, it means complete work satisfaction. Your occupation ceases to be thought of as "work" because it becomes a pleasure. How nice to be paid to do something that you so enjoy!

WUNJO indicates a happy outcome to any problem that you may have. An excellent omen in a spread, especially if it comes in the "result" position.

When combined with travel Runes like RAIDO and EHWAZ, it forecasts a successful journey or a vacation. Finalize plans as soon as possible.

Teamed with a message Rune like ANSUZ, WUNJO signifies good news coming to you by mail or telephone. That long-awaited confirmation or contract, perhaps!

With love-related Runes, such as FEHU, it indicates true love and a lasting relationship. If you make positive overtures now they will be well-received.

If your question concerns health, WUNJO is a superb harbinger, especially when linked with KAUNAZ.

SUMMARY
* Good news * Contentment *
* Achievement * Positive outcome *
* Travel * Loving relationships *
* Improved health *

WUNJO ON A RUNIC CLOTH:

- IN EARTH: Be grateful to be alive. Covert thoughts should be avoided. They can only mar your new-found happiness.

- IN FIRE: A problem shared is a problem halved. Seek the advice of a friend and thus make the most of this favorable sign.

- IN AIR: Happiness, long overdue, is about to descend on you! Don't let it overwhelm you – enjoy it!

- IN WATER: Be mindful of the plight of others. The route to your own happiness lies there. Charity may begin at home but it should not end there.

WUNJO REVERSED:

- Most of the WUNJO upright indications become opposite in meaning when WUNJO is reversed – especially in the "result" position. It is not that things *will be* opposite – merely a warning that if you don't take sufficient care, things *could* become a little difficult. Watch your health, particularly your chest. Check and double-check any travel arrangements you may have made.

- Do everything you can to delay finalizing any legal or other commitments until a more favorable time. WUNJO can also be a warning to remain mentally sober! Don't get carried away with your apparent invulnerability at this time.

9. HAGALAZ

Keyword: CHAOS   Element: WATER

Meaning: **Hail, frost** ✳ *Deity:* **Heimdall**
✳ *Direction:* **West** ✳ *Animal:* **Serpent** ✳ *Color:* **White**
✳ *Tree:* **Yew** ✳ *Herb:* **Briony**

- HAGALAZ portends disruption of your carefully made plans. You will probably have to rearrange your schedule to a more favorable time.

- Certain limitations will be placed upon you.

- Your frustration will be almost unbearable, but HAGALAZ urges you to be patient – to bide your time. The forces working against you at the moment come from a totally unexpected source and are completely beyond your control.

- Although the delays will be annoying, they do not mean that you need to sit around like a couch-potato. This is a good time to reassess your position and clarify your thoughts.

- Exercise caution at all times.

- Be prepared for surprises – possibly unpleasant ones. HAGALAZ gives you this warning so that you can take evasive action, roll with the punches, and (later) come fighting back!

- There is a chance that a calculated risk could reap you rich benefits. Even if you are 200% sure, wait until the mood changes in your favor. Then you can release the shackles that have been restricting your creative flow. Be ever-mindful that an unforeseen counterattack could still wound you.

- Don't fight the unfightable.

SUMMARY
* Disruptions * Limitations *
* Frustrations * Reassessment *
* Caution * Surprises *
* Inevitability *

HAGALAZ ON A RUNIC CLOTH:

ᚺ IN EARTH: Caution is called for. Advance with small steps and test the ground thoroughly before you tread on it. Be circumspect.

ᚺ IN FIRE: Watch out! There is trouble about. Avoid scandal and, above all, don't get involved in other people's dramas. You have a starring part in your own drama at present!

ᚺ IN AIR: Powerful currents are influencing your life, over which you have no control.

ᚺ IN WATER: Take great care over everything you do. Negative forces abound at present, so keep a low profile.

ᚺ HAGALAZ has no reversed aspect.

10. NAUTHIZ

Keyword: NEEDS   Element: FIRE

> *Meaning:* **Need** ✳ *Deity:* **Frigga**
> ✳ *Direction:* **South** ✳ *Color:* **Blue** ✳ *Tree:* **Beech**
> ✳ *Herb:* **Snakeweed**

ᛉ Constraint is called for by the appearance of NAUTHIZ. It reflects your needs rather than your desires.

ᛉ This is a time to revaluate the current situation so that your future success can be assured.

ᛉ It is not a time for gambling of any kind. You will be unlucky at cards *and* unlucky in love, if you gamble.

ᛉ Avoid anything that appears to be a bargain – or a money-making scheme that appears to be foolproof. It won't be! Disappointment can only follow.

ᛉ NAUTHIZ suggests that patience is the correct approach to take while striving to reach your goals, because delays seem inevitable.

ᛉ It also indicates a lowering of resistance to minor illnesses. Take care not to overextend yourself. This is no time to burn the candle at both ends!

ᛉ It is a difficult time for you romantically, because you feel that you are not being fully appreciated or satisfied.

ᛉ You will come through this period of time having learned some valuable lessons in self-control. These lessons will greatly assist you to conquer your adversities when the time is more fortuitous.

ᛉ Are you by any chance making a mountain out of a molehill?

SUMMARY
* *Constraint* * *Revaluation* *
* *Disappointment* * *Patience* *
* *Inevitable delays* *
* *Low resistance* * *Self-control* *

NAUTHIZ ON A RUNIC CLOTH:

ᚾ IN EARTH: Think before you act. Prudence and patience will never be more important to you.

ᚾ IN FIRE: There are difficult times ahead. Don't be downhearted, because your patience and confidence will see you through.

ᚾ IN AIR: A major task cannot be put off any longer. You must face up to it. You will need boundless energy to complete it. Don't be in too much of a hurry, though, or your health may suffer.

ᚾ IN WATER: Difficulties are approaching. Remain steadfast and your success will be assured.

NAUTHIZ REVERSED:

ᚾ Definitely a sign that you should exercise caution. You would be well-advised to wait for a more favorable moment to undertake anything of importance to you. Any snap judgment would probably be regretted.

ᚾ This is also an indication that you should be more realistic in the goals that you have set yourself. If you are already involved in a plan that seems to be sinking fast, you should accept the loss to your pocket and your pride and quit now!

11. ISA

Keyword: STANDSTILL Element: WATER

Meaning: **Ice** * *Deity:* **Skadi** * *Direction:* **North**
* *Animal:* **Reindeer** * *Color:* **Black**
* *Tree:* **Alder** * *Herb:* **Henbane**

This is the "ice" Rune. Like ice, it indicates that your actions are, or should be, frozen.

Psychological blocks to activity and thought exist and are bearing down upon the present situation. You need to exercise great patience and show philosophical understanding.

Temporary parting, of a business or family nature, could be indicated.

You will probably be called upon to make sacrifices at this time and submit to the inevitable.

With all your exciting plans "on hold," you will benefit by waiting for a more favorable time before forging ahead.

A wait that is forced upon you could turn out to be very beneficial to you in the future, because it will give you an uncalled-for but most welcome chance to revaluate the problem. You will probably discover facets of it that were invisible to you until now.

ISA has chosen this as a period of cooling down.

Any emotive ideas that you have need to be controlled. Wait for the other person to make the first move.

SUMMARY
* *Standstill* * *Psychological blocks* *
* *Patience* * *Sacrifices* * *Waiting* *
* *Control* * *Cooling-down period* *
* *Isolation* *

ISA ON A RUNIC CLOTH:

| IN EARTH: You must be prepared for some disappointments. Psychologically, this is a tense time for you.

| IN FIRE: Great caution should be exercised now, because many dangerous influences surround you.

| IN AIR: Now is the time for extreme caution because of surrounding danger

| IN WATER: These could be difficult times for you, so exercise patience.

| ISA has no reversed aspect.

12. JERA

Keyword: FRUITFULNESS   Element: EARTH

> *Meaning:* **Harvest** ✳ *Deity:* **Frey/Freya**
> ✳ *Direction:* **North** ✳ *Bird:* **Goose** ✳ *Color:* **Brown**
> ✳ *Tree:* **Oak** ✳ *Herb:* **Rosemary**

⟡ JERA in your Rune cast is a sign that you will reap the benefits of your efforts. Tasks that need completing and contracts that need finalizing get the "green light" at this time.

⟡ This Rune is a symbol of slow but steady improvement over the next year. Like the four seasons, your life will be subject to gradual changes, but with a distinct improvement in your financial situation as the end result.

⟡ These changes will probably occur without necessitating any further effort on your part. JERA shows the "harvesting" of seeds that you have already sown.

⟡ It is a sign of psychological peace and tranquil prosperity, a time to look at situations philosophically and examine your roots. Don't try to fight the basic instincts that you may be feeling.

⟡ Relax and let your emotions follow the natural channels that will bring you closer to the time-honored forces of nature.

⟡ Sometimes JERU will signify that a lawyer or legal matters have a bearing on this period.

⟡ Look, listen, and learn.

SUMMARY
* Rewarded efforts *
* Steady improvement *
* Gradual changes *
* Psychological peace *
* Tranquil prosperity *
* Legal matters *

JERA ON A RUNIC CLOTH:

- ◊ IN EARTH: A calm, steady period. Try to relax. Too much effort is counterproductive. Avoid arguments and new experiments.

- ◊ IN FIRE: Success is coming but quite slowly. Face up to the realities of life and don't run away from your problems.

- ◊ IN AIR: Be patient. Remain calm and avoid confrontations. After delays, things will go well again.

- ◊ IN WATER: Be careful. Stay calm and unemotional. Try to anticipate the long-term effect of the choices that you are considering making.

- ◊ JERA has no reversed aspect.

13. EIHWAZ

Keyword: TOGETHERNESS   Element: EARTH

Meaning: **Yew tree** ✳ *Deity:* **Ull/Odin**
✳ *Direction:* **North** ✳ *Color:* **Green** ✳ *Tree:* **Yew**
✳ *Herb:* **Briony**

ᛇ EIHWAZ symbolizes difficulties that will require extreme tact and diplomacy to overcome. It is a time to be on your guard and to build up your inner strengths.

ᛇ It is also a sign that things will improve after a short delay that could prove beneficial.

ᛇ Try to anticipate – look ahead – and see your problems before they mature into real headaches! The strength of EIHWAZ will guide you. Look at the surrounding Runes to give you an accurate direction for your concerted efforts.

ᛇ A time to utilize all your skills together to establish the foundations for lasting future development. Your plans are realistic and can be achieved, but you must think before you act.

ᛇ A problem that may have existed for a long while will be successfully resolved.

ᛇ As the yew tree is a sure sign of protection, EIHWAZ is in many ways a fortunate Rune to draw: an "insurance" for the successful outcome of a project or plan.

ᛇ News from the past could well affect you at this time.

SUMMARY
* *Difficulties requiring tact* *
* *Beneficial delays to plans* *
* *Renewed effort and determination* *
* *Realistic plans* *
* *Protection* *

EIHWAZ ON A RUNIC CLOTH:

- IN EARTH: Clarity of thought is called for. You must remain unaffected by infuriating influences. Stay calm and solid as the trunk of the yew tree.

- IN FIRE: Face up to your problems. This is not the time to hide behind a curtain.

- IN AIR: Avoid getting involved in arguments. Be calm and collected.

- IN WATER: Keep your thoughts to yourself. Diplomacy is called for. Show outward calm and control, no matter what you may feel inside.

- EIHWAZ has no reversed aspect.

14. PERTHO

Keyword: MYSTERY　　Element: WATER

Meaning: **Birth/the womb** ✳ *Deity:* **Frigg**
✳ *Direction:* **Northeast** ✳ *Bird:* **Heron** ✳ *Color:* **Red**
✳ *Tree:* **Beech** ✳ *Herb:* **Aconite**

When PERTHO appears in your Rune cast, you are working with powerful forces in your favor. Your hidden and latent talents will come to the fore and could bring you unexpected financial gains.

PERTHO indicates that you could be "initiated" into an entirely new project or hobby.

This is a sign of revelations and secrets being revealed to you. Many surprises and unforeseen turns of events, of a fortuitous nature, are indicated.

You will feel the full force of your psychic ability coming into play in the "game of life." A wonderful period for spiritual development.

There could possibly be news from afar and a joyful reunion with an old friend.

If you have mislaid an object, it will be found. If you are inquiring about a nagging problem, the solution will be revealed to you.

PERTHO symbolizes fate – yet fate working for you to bring extreme happiness. It has intense sensual, sexual, and occult connotations.

> **SUMMARY**
> ✳ *Spiritual and occult development* ✳
> ✳ *Financial gain* ✳ *New projects* ✳
> ✳ *Favorable outcomes directed by uncontrollable forces* ✳ *Reunions* ✳
> *Solutions* ✳ *Favorable time for personal relationships* ✳

PERTHO ON A RUNIC CLOTH:

⌐ IN EARTH: Be aware of your surroundings. Take care and watch out for possible sources of trouble.

⌐ IN FIRE: Think before you speak. You can't trust anybody. Keep your opinions to yourself.

⌐ IN AIR: A very fortunate period for you. You are about to experience pleasant surprises.

⌐ IN WATER: A time to avoid taking risks or gambles of any kind. New ventures should not be entered into just yet.

PERTHO REVERSED:

⌐ Slight disappointments and a lessening of your goals are indicated.

Take great care, because if you have any guilty secrets, they could surface embarrassingly. Keep a tight hold on your purse-strings. You should definitely not gamble or lend money at this time, because such a move would probably end in tears.

⌐ Don't be too disheartened. PERTHO REVERSED should be considered a friendly warning not to take anything for granted at this time and to be especially vigilant for possible antagonistic influences.

15. ALGIZ

Keyword: DEFENSE   Element: AIR

Meaning: **Protection** ✳ *Deity:* **Heimdall**
✳ *Direction:* **Northeast** ✳ *Animal:* **Elk** ✳ *Color:* **Purple**
✳ *Tree:* **Yew** ✳ *Herb:* **Sedge**

ᛉ ALGIZ, especially in the "result" position, signifies assistance given to you when you least expect it – from someone who is usually unsympathetic. Accept the help, because it will be offered unconditionally.

ᛉ This is a time to persevere with your plans and to stick by your principles in an uncompromising manner. The power of ALGIZ will support you in all your ventures. There could be real and worthwhile career opportunities at this time.

ᛉ The fortunate new influences that ALGIZ showers upon you could make you feel complacent. Don't be lulled into a state of slothfulness just because everything is going so well. ALGIZ does not suffer fools gladly. Go all out to achieve your goals but keep a clear eye and an alert mind at all times.

ᛉ You could well be overwhelmed by the hospitality of friends and have difficulty fitting all your appointments into your social calendar.

ᛉ ALGIZ is also a sign of continued good health, or a curative period leading to renewed health.

ᛉ You will have premonitions of possible dangers, and these will be pinpointed by the other Runes in the cast.

SUMMARY
* Unexpected assistance *
* Career opportunities * Perseverance *
* Fortunate new influences *
* Danger of complacence *
* Successful social life * Good health *
* Strong psychic period with
many premonitions *

ALGIZ ON A RUNIC CLOTH:

ᛦ IN EARTH: Watch your back, because someone could be trying to deceive you. Remain alert, because you are vulnerable.

ᛦ IN FIRE: A time to be outgoing, extroverted, and magnanimous. A time to share yourself with your friends – to accept and give invitations.

ᛦ IN AIR: The moment of truth is at hand. After careful consideration you must finally make up your mind and inform those who are concerned.

ᛦ IN WATER: Things are definitely going your way, so expansion could be called for. Go for it!

ALGIZ REVERSED:

ᛘ This is a sign that you are vulnerable at present. You may have to make a sacrifice, and any "chancy" proposition should be avoided.

ᛘ The advice of others should be investigated thoroughly before you commit yourself, because deception is clearly indicated. If in doubt – do nothing!

ᛘ There could also be a touch of self-deception indicated, brought about by complacency.

ᛘ Nobody likes to be blamed for something that they haven't done. Be especially aware – because injustices are part of the ALGIZ REVERSED symbolism.

16. SOWULO

Keyword: ENTHUSIASM   Element: AIR

Meaning: **Sun** ✳ *Deity:* **Balder**
✳ *Direction:* **Northeast** ✳ *Bird:* **Eagle**
✳ *Color:* **Yellow** ✳ *Tree:* **Juniper** ✳ *Herb:* **Mistletoe**

⌇ It is indeed a fortunate omen when SOWULO appears in your Rune cast.

⌇ It is a sign of victory, conquest, and success against all the odds. Definite progress is assured.

⌇ SOWULO indicates vigor – so naturally it foretells a time of robust good health and quick recovery from any illness.

⌇ Strong sexual connotations are also connected to this Rune, so – if you were previously fainthearted – you should now take your courage in both hands and claim what is rightfully yours.

⌇ SOWULO shows the triumph of good over bad, strong over weak, good over evil. Any opposition that you encounter will, therefore, swiftly be overcome.

⌇ Travel, of both a business and private nature, could also be indicated.

⌇ The only danger when SOWULO appears in your Rune cast is that sometimes it warns that you are overdoing things. Be careful not to drive yourself too hard.

SUMMARY
✳ Victory ✳ Conquest ✳ Success ✳
✳ Vigor ✳ Good health ✳
✳ Sexuality ✳
✳ Triumph over adversity ✳
✳ Travel ✳
✳ Overwork ✳

SOWULO ON A RUNIC CLOTH:

↯ IN EARTH: Careful consideration of all matters is called for. Whatever happens, you must remain cool, calm, and collected!

↯ IN FIRE: Count to ten before you do or say anything. Try not to be provoked into hasty action.

↯ IN AIR: You could benefit from relaxing your grip on the reins for a while. You possibly need to recharge your batteries.

↯ IN WATER: Slow but steady progress will reap benefits later on. A time to exercise patience.

↯ SOWULO has no reversed aspect.

17. TEIWAZ

Keyword: ZEST Element: AIR

Meaning: **Victory** ✳ *Deity:* **Tyr**
✳ *Direction:* **East** ✳ *Color:* **Red** ✳ *Tree:* **Oak**
✳ *Herb:* **Sage**

↑ An adventurous time could well be forthcoming, because TEIWAZ indicates that this is a good moment to venture forward. Those menial tasks that you have been dreading or avoiding should be tackled now. They will seem easy now that the force of TEIWAZ is working for you. You will wonder what you were frightened about!

↑ TEIWAZ is a sign that you should be bold and courageous. Everything should be undertaken with a driving passion.

↑ Any legal matter will have a successful outcome. You should see an increase in income or power as a reward for your efforts.

↑ This is an extremely happy time for personal relationships. Your love will be returned.

↑ If you are seeking help regarding a matter of health, you should stop worrying, because TEIWAZ is a sign of rapid recovery from illness.

↑ It also signifies leadership and authority. It may be that this Rune is urging you to accept more responsibility and get fuller recognition for your talents and efforts.

↑ A time to assess your abilities, take stock of your alternatives – then go for gold!

SUMMARY
* Adventure *
* Attack outstanding problems *
* Passionate motivation *
* Legal success * Loving personal relationships * Responsibility *
* Deserved rewards *

TEIWAZ ON A RUNIC CLOTH:

↑ IN EARTH: Show your inner feelings and speak your mind. People will appreciate your frankness. Have the courage to show that you are sensitive.

↑ IN FIRE: Changes are called for, so don't be frightened to try out something new. There is a need for rejuvenation in many aspects of your life.

↑ IN AIR: Delays in your plans would promote unnecessary problems – so you must act decisively if you are to achieve your goals.

↑ IN WATER: Don't stay in a rut. Think about your situation and then opt for change. There is always more than one solution to a problem, and new ideas could prove best for you.

TEIWAZ REVERSED:

↓ A frustrating sign of stagnation. This sometimes indicates a loss, or a snag arising in an emotional or business relationship. You should be particularly attentive to your loved ones if TEIWAZ REVERSED appears, because it often signifies that you have been inattentive of late and that your partner feels neglected.

↓ There is a tremendous energy block in force at present. TEIWAZ REVERSED advises you to remain patient. The game of life will soon turn full circle for you.

18. BERKANA

Keyword: NEW BEGINNINGS   Element: EARTH

Meaning: **Growth** ✳ *Deity:* **Holda**
✳ *Direction:* **East** ✳ *Animal:* **Bear** ✳ *Bird:* **Swan**
✳ *Color:* **Blue** ✳ *Tree:* **Birch** ✳ *Herb:* **Lady's-mantle**

ᛒ BERKANA is the major Rune of creativity. Birth of children, or new ideas, is clearly represented. A marriage or remarriage could well be in the offing – again, either of a personal or business nature.

ᛒ A fertile mind in a fertile body means that this will be a very stimulating and exciting time for you. Numerous ideas will be considered, and BERKANA will look favorably upon any new ventures that you undertake.

ᛒ This Rune signifies that you should keep an eye on existing projects and relationships, too. They may be in need of a little nurturing at this time until they are strong enough to stand up on their own again – just like the potted plant that needs to be watered regularly!

ᛒ If your are asking the Runes about "children," then BERKANA in your Rune cast is a most favorable omen. It signifies that the time is right for passing on your values and knowledge to your siblings.

ᛒ BERKANA is a "health" Rune – and in the upright position it is a sign of continued good health or quick recovery from an illness. It is a most favorable Rune and should be treated with great respect.

SUMMARY
* Creativity * Partnerships *
* Stimulation * Excitement *
* Awareness * Teaching *
* Caring * Good health *

BERKANA ON A RUNIC CLOTH:

ᛒ **IN EARTH:** Hold back a little. Try not to be too pushy, because things could rebound on you.

ᛒ **IN FIRE:** Attention to detail is called for, if you are going to get full advantage from the present favorable conditions.

ᛒ **IN AIR:** Exciting family news is quite probable. A birth or a new venture is a distinct possibility.

ᛒ **IN WATER:** This is a time for self-assessment, so relax and count your blessings!

BERKANA REVERSED:

ᛥ Take great care at home because family upheaval, disagreements, or anxieties show. Your plans could well be on hold, and partnerships, both business and personal, could become a little suspect.

ᛥ Pay particular attention to your health, because you could well be vulnerable at this time.

ᛥ Hold out for your rights and principles, as the tide will soon turn in your favor again.

19. EHWAZ

Keyword: ADVENTURE   Element: EARTH

Meaning: **Horse** ✳ *Deity:* **Frey/Freya**
✳ *Direction:* **East** ✳ *Animal:* **Horse** ✳ *Color:* **White** ✳
Tree: **Oak** ✳ *Herb:* **Ragwort**

ᛗ Movement and change are signified when EHWAZ appears for you. This could involve your house or job, or just plans in general terms.

ᛗ Be prepared for new beginnings, which could signify travel to faraway places. There is certainly an exciting time ahead for you, and you can be quietly confident that you will succeed in these new ventures. You are warned, however, not to show too much outward confidence because of the real danger that someone might come along and defeat you at the last moment. You would have only yourself to blame.

ᛗ EHWAZ is a good portent for relationships of a personal and sexual nature. It is an indication that partnerships are more likely to succeed than solo efforts.

ᛗ Cooperation and adaptability are definitely called for.

ᛗ EHWAZ brings confirmation and emphasis to the surrounding Runes in the divination spread. It acts like an "insurance" card!

SUMMARY
* Movement * Travel *
* Confidence * Excitement *
* Cooperation * Adaptability *
* Sensuality *

EHWAZ ON A RUNIC CLOTH:

ᛗ IN EARTH: A new and important person will emerge who could be of great assistance to you.

ᛗ IN FIRE: Play your cards close to your chest, and keep your emotions and thoughts to yourself.

ᛗ IN AIR: Consider the spiritual answer to your problem. Possibly you are giving too much prominence to the material and transitory aspects of life.

ᛗ IN WATER: A time to be courageous and to act with force, after considering your options.

EHWAZ REVERSED:

ᛞ The power of EHWAZ becomes only slightly less formidable when it is reversed. It is, however, a sign that you should keep your emotions in check and be mindful of other people's feelings – even though this could cause you frustration.

20. MANNAZ

Keyword: HUMANITY　　Element: AIR

> *Meaning:* **Man** ✳ *Deity:* **Heimdall**
> ✳ *Direction:* **Southeast** ✳ *Animal:* **Man** ✳ *Bird:* **Hawk**
> ✳ *Color:* **Purple** ✳ *Tree:* **Holly** ✳ *Herb:* **Madder**

ᛗ MANNAZ is a sign of unity and of family ties. This is not a time to go it alone! The assistance of your nearest and dearest will be a great comfort to you – indeed, it is essential that you take advantage of the protection they afford.

ᛗ Changes in employment, habitat, or direction seem imminent, but these changes have been planned and will not come as a surprise to you.

ᛗ MANNAZ shows steady progress and overdue success just around the corner.

ᛗ You may need to seek the advice of another person who is not kith or kin. If the person is unknown to you, proceed with great care, because the indications are that deception is afoot! This could concern a conflict with authority.

ᛗ This Rune suggests that you should remain modest about your abilities and achievements in order to avoid possible jealousy from your associates.

SUMMARY
✳ *Family unity and assistance* ✳
✳ *Change in direction* ✳
✳ *Steady progress* ✳
✳ *Overdue success* ✳ *Deception* ✳
✳ *Authoritarianism* ✳ *Jealousies* ✳
✳ *Modesty* ✳

MANNAZ ON A RUNIC CLOTH:

ᛗ **IN EARTH:** You must pace yourself. There is danger in pressing too hard and too soon. Failure will result.

ᛗ **IN FIRE:** Treasure your relationships and family ties. They are very strong and you must work to strengthen them even further.

ᛗ **IN AIR:** Antagonism is in the air! Be like the duck who lets the water roll off its back – remain uninvolved.

ᛗ **IN WATER:** Someone close to you could be plotting against you. Have you offended a friend or acquaintance?

MANNAZ REVERSED:

ᛦ You are out on your own again, but without the help of others. Changes should be postponed, if possible. Difficulties will confront you and many stumbling blocks could impede your progress.

ᛦ Keep your emotions in check. This is the worst time to show your frustrations. Reassess your situation and count your blessings.

21. LAGUZ

Keyword: INTUITION   Element: WATER

Meaning: **Lake** * *Deity:* **Njord/Nerthus**
* *Direction:* **Southeast** * *Animal:* **Seal** * *Bird:* **Gull**
* *Color:* **Green** * *Tree:* **Osier** * *Herb:* **Leek**

LAGUZ stands for the free flow of creative and intuitive ideas. If you are torn between two different courses of action, you should follow your nose! Don't be swayed by the opinions of others. Go your own way if you desire to be successful.

Nobody knows your own problems better than you do, so be courageous – make your decision and stick by it. You are being guided by a Higher Force, which is your insurance!

Your intuition could warn you of a possible source of danger or setback. Heed your "gut feelings" and take appropriate evasive action. Be firm but fair.

LAGUZ is one of the travel Runes – especially where water is concerned. So a long journey overseas may be imminent.

Do you have a rare – maybe an academic – hobby or interest? LAGUZ signifies success in this direction, possibly even financial success.

This Rune also indicates that the tide has finally turned in your favor and that you will be able to see the light at the end of the tunnel at last.

SUMMARY
* Intuition * Creativity *
* Courageous action *
* Dynamic decisions *
* Dangers averted * Travel *
* Academic success *
* Good change in fortunes *

LAGUZ ON A RUNIC CLOTH:

- IN EARTH: Look to the spiritual "you." Search beneath the surface for your answers and don't push your fears and desires to the back of the drawer of life!

- IN FIRE: Although you can learn from the past, you must not live in it! Look to the future for your answers and heed your own intuitiveness.

- IN AIR: There may be a solution to your problem that is not immediately obvious to you: a hidden secret. The Runes reveal hidden secrets.

- IN WATER: Certain things are hidden from you – so don't be complacent. Think very carefully before you act.

LAGUZ REVERSED:

- This is usually a bad or warning sign – unless it is accompanied by more favorable Runes.

- Temptations surround you, and yet you must take care not to offend with your refusal.

- You could benefit from the opinions of a friend, whose advice should not be ignored. Be prepared for the possibility that your plan will fail.

- LAGUZ REVERSED often foretells of the danger of excess.

22. INGUZ

Keyword: ACHIEVEMENT   Element: EARTH

> *Meaning:* **Genitals** ✳ *Deity:* **Frey/Freya** ✳ *Direction:*
> **Southeast** ✳ *Animal:* **Boar** ✳ *Bird:* **Cuckoo**
> ✳ *Color:* **Black** ✳ *Tree:* **Apple** ✳ *Herb:* **Camomile**

◊ INGUZ is symbolic of both the male and female genitals and is, therefore, a potent sign of fertility. "A fertile mind in a fertile body" is a succinct way to express the true meaning of this Rune.

◊ Difficult tasks will be successfully completed.

◊ Apparently insolvable problems will suddenly become solvable – the answer so apparent that you will wonder why you hadn't reached the conclusion before.

◊ This Rune often heralds a time for relaxation – a vacation, perhaps. Relax in the firm knowledge that all is right in your world at the moment, so you can afford the time out to recharge your batteries.

◊ When INGUZ appears in the "result" position in your cast, one of its most beneficial side effects is that it indicates the immediate easing of a stressful situation and progression to a more stable one.

◊ INGUZ could also signify a significant and beneficial change in your life. The surrounding Runes will show you where this change is likely to come from.

> **SUMMARY**
> ✳ *Fertile mind and body* ✳
> ✳ *Completion* ✳ *Success* ✳
> ✳ *Relaxation* ✳ *Easing of stress* ✳
> ✳ *Change for the good* ✳

INGUZ ON A RUNIC CLOTH:

- ⋄ IN EARTH: You have to change if you are to succeed in your task. You must be forward-thinking and not rest on your laurels, otherwise your mission will fail.

- ⋄ IN FIRE: It is better to give than to receive. This is never truer than now, because selfishness will mean your ultimate downfall.

- ⋄ IN AIR: Take notice of the opinions of others. There could be good sense in their ideas, and you could benefit from their experiences.

- ⋄ IN WATER: Other people hold the key to your destiny. It is a time to trust them – this is your best option at the moment.

- ⋄ INGUZ has no reversed aspect.

23. OTHILA

Keyword: SECURITY   Element: EARTH

Meaning: **Inherited land** ✳ *Deity:* **Odin**
✳ *Direction:* **South** ✳ *Color:* **Brown**
✳ *Tree:* **Hawthorn** ✳ *Herb:* **Clover**

⋋ OTHILA is a sign that new directions should be taken and a more up-to-date stance adopted. The past separates from the present in a way that broadens your attitudes.

⋋ Strong powers are working to help create wealth and prosperity for you. This appears to be inherited wealth as opposed to earned wealth. This could be in the form of property.

⋋ You will become aware of the tremendous responsibility that you bear in administering and caring for that which is in your trust.

⋋ If you have children, they will need your special attention at this time.

⋋ Although new directions are signposted, there has never been a more important time for honoring and acknowledging the efforts of your ancestors.

⋋ This is a period of moral and spiritual revival. A search for *the* truth! You will derive great benefit from this, and your partner could well acquire a better understanding and appreciation of you as a result of your new-found mental and metaphysical clarity.

SUMMARY
* *New directions and attitudes* *
* *Inherited wealth* * *Prosperity* *
* *Family responsibility* *
* *Moral and spiritual revival* *

OTHILA ON A RUNIC CLOTH:

- ᛟ IN EARTH: Your perseverance will reap rewards. Keep at it, because other people depend on your wisdom.

- ᛟ IN FIRE: Building a home or business takes time. Proceed with renewed vigor – but be patient.

- ᛟ IN AIR: Put your family and home *first*. This is not a time to be selfish! Your generosity will be appreciated.

- ᛟ IN WATER: Success seems assured – if you are prepared to take a risk! Open up a bit and show that you mean business.

OTHILA REVERSED:

- ᛟ A bad time to try to change the world! Any effort on your part to go against accepted protocol can only meet with embarrassment and failure.

- ᛟ OTHILA REVERSED signifies possible opposition, legal and financial disputes.

24. **DAGAZ**

Keyword: LIFE   Element: FIRE

Meaning: **Day** ✳ *Deity:* **Heimdall** ✳ *Direction:* **South** ✳ *Animal:* **Cat** ✳ *Bird:* **Swallow** ✳ *Color:* **Yellow** ✳ *Tree:* **Spruce** ✳ *Herb:* **Clary sage**

⋈ DAGAZ sheds new light on your problems, indicating breakthrough and a transformation of your fortunes.

⋈ Drawing this Rune could signify a dramatic change in your life. You are asked to go along with this and to accept the inevitable. The change will be to your advantage.

⋈ Seemingly impenetrable barriers will be broken down at last to create a wonderful atmosphere of relief and freedom.

⋈ You will feel that a great weight has been lifted off your shoulders.

⋈ Do not hesitate to act *now!* The power of DAGAZ is with you.

⋈ You should succeed – even if you find that the odds are stacked against you.

⋈ DAGAZ encourages you to act "intuitively" – to have the courage of your convictions and "go for it!" The progress will be slow but, nevertheless, considerable.

SUMMARY
* Breakthrough * Transformation *
* Dramatic change * Relief *
* Freedom *
* Success against the odds *
* Progress *

DAGAZ ON A RUNIC CLOTH:

- ⋈ IN EARTH: Every minute of the day will present you with opportunities. Take advantage of them all.

- ⋈ IN FIRE: Don't act until tomorrow. The tide is about to turn in your direction – so don't be in too much of a hurry.

- ⋈ IN AIR: You need to think before you act. DAGAZ in Air is a directive to hold your counsel.

- ⋈ IN WATER: There is no better time to act than *now!* This day – this minute – this second!

- ⋈ DAGAZ has no reversed aspect.

25. **WYRD**

"In the lap of the gods"

> *I am sure that there are times in our lives when we are not meant to know how things will turn out. We have to be patient and await the eventual outcome.*

- WYRD (pronounced "weird") represents this unknown factor. When you draw this Rune, it signifies that the final result is dependant on *fate alone*. The answer that you seek is unknown, undecided, unclear, and has yet to be resolved. We have no right to know the answer at this moment!

- This is the Rune of *total trust.* Its blankness symbolizes death – not in the ultimate sense, but as a signal that changes are afoot, although not just yet! The old will eventually make way for the new. It mirrors your doubts and uncertainties.

- WYRD challenges your faith. It may call you to sail across uncharted waters and confront... who knows what?

- Although fate cannot be "controlled," it can be influenced slightly! The neighboring Runes in your spread will advise you on an appropriate course of action to help make the "unknowable" at least a little more "favorable."

- WYRD is a comparative newcomer to the Rune family. Nevertheless, it should be treated with great respect. It should not be discarded in the way that you would discard a joker from a standard pack of playing cards. WYRD is not a joker. It interrelates with its companions to create a wonderfully magical environment and helps oil the cogs that make the Rune machine function correctly.

- You must have the courage to face the changes that are about to occur. Accept responsibility for your previous actions.

- If you are seeking information about someone else, the appearance of WYRD in your Rune cast will be a sign that you had better mind your own business and not interfere with things that don't concern you.

- WYRD can be positive as well as negative. If it is linked with positive or love runes, such as GEBO, JERA, BERKANA, and INGUZ, it could indicate that a new partnership of some sort will shortly be entered into, with exciting but as yet unknown consequences.

- WYRD has no reversed aspect.

SUMMARY

FREYR'S AETT	HAGAL'S AETT	TYR'S AETT
1. Fehu	*9*. Hagalaz	*17*. Teiwaz
2. Uruz	*10*. Nauthiz	*18*. Berkana
3. Thurisaz	*11*. Isa	*19*. Ehwaz
4. Ansuz	*12*. Jera	*20*. Mannaz
5. Raido	*13*. Eihwaz	*21*. Laguz
6. Kenaz	*14*. Pertho	*22*. Inguz
7. Gebo	*15*. Algiz	*23*. Othila
8. Wunjo	*16*. Sowulo	*24*. Dagaz

25. Wyrd